The Primary Source Library of Famous Composers ™

Ludwig van Beethoven

Eric Michael Summerer

The Rosen Publishing Group's

PowerKids Press ™

PRIMARY SOURCE

New York

To Stefanie

Published in 2006 by The Rosen Publishing Group, Inc.
29 East 21st Street, New York, NY 10010

First Edition

Editor: Frances E. Ruffin
Book Design: Michael J. Caroleo

Eric "Michaels" Summerer is Music Director and the "morning guy" at the Internet radio station Beethoven.com

Photo Credits: Cover (Beethoven) © Snark/Art Resource, NY; cover and interior borders (sheet music) Library of Congress, Music Division; p. 4 Beethoven-Haus, Bonn, Germany / Bridgeman Art Library; pp. 6 (left), 20 (bottom) © Erich Lessing/Art Resource, NY; pp. 6–7 (bottom) © Hulton/Archive/Getty Images; p. 7 (right) Private Collection/Roger-Viollet, Paris/Bridgeman Art Library; pp. 8, 19 (left) Historisches Museum der Stadt, Vienna, Austria / Bridgeman Art Library; pp. 11, 16, 19 (right), 23 © Bettman/Corbis; p. 12 The Art Archive/Museum der Stadt Wien/Dagli Orti; p. 15 The Art Archive/Beethoven Museum Bonn/Dagli Orti; p. 20 (left) Time Life Pictures/Getty Images; p. 20 (right) Kunsthistorisches Museum, Vienna, Austria / Bridgeman Art Library; pp. 24 (music), 27 Beethoven Haus, Bonn/Giraudon/Bridgeman Art Library; p. 24 (portrait) Beethoven-Haus Bonn.

Library of Congress Cataloging-in-Publication Data

Summerer, Eric Michael.
Ludwig van Beethoven / Eric Michael Summerer.
    p. cm. — (The primary source library of famous composers)
Summary: Introduces Ludwig van Beethoven, one of the best-known composers of all time, who not only broke the rules about how music is written, but also about how musicians should be treated.
Includes bibliographical references (p.   ) and index.
ISBN 1-4042-2771-7 (lib. bdg.)
1. Beethoven, Ludwig van, 1770–1827—Juvenile literature. 2. Composers—Austria—Biography—Juvenile literature. [1. Beethoven, Ludwig van, 1770–1827. 2. Composers.] I. Title. II. Series.
ML3930.B4 S85 2005
780'.92—dc22

                                          2003015451

Manufactured in the United States of America

Contents

The Great Beethoven

Many people believe that Ludwig van Beethoven was the greatest **composer** who ever lived. Music lovers around the world perform and enjoy Beethoven's best-known work. Beethoven wrote music for many different instruments. He liked to break the rules when it came to **classical music**. He wrote music that was different from what others wrote. He also felt that **musicians** should be treated better than they were treated at the time. During the 1700s and the 1800s, musicians were considered servants, part of a social class that was lower than that of the **aristocrats** who ruled Europe. Beethoven did not agree. He once told his **patron** Prince Lichnowsky, "There are and there will be thousands of princes. There is only one Beethoven."

In this picture, done in the 1800s, Beethoven is in his early fifties. He is shown composing the Missa Solemnis, which was the Mass in D.

A Musical Family

Ludwig van Beethoven was born into a musical family in Bonn, Germany. We do not know the exact date of Beethoven's birth, but he was **baptized** on December 17, 1770. His grandfather, also named Ludwig, was a **court** musician who played the **organ** and sang. Beethoven's father, Johann, was the kapellmeister, or music director, for the court **orchestra** of an important church leader

Beethoven was named for his grandfather, Ludwig, who is shown here. Ludwig was a court musician.

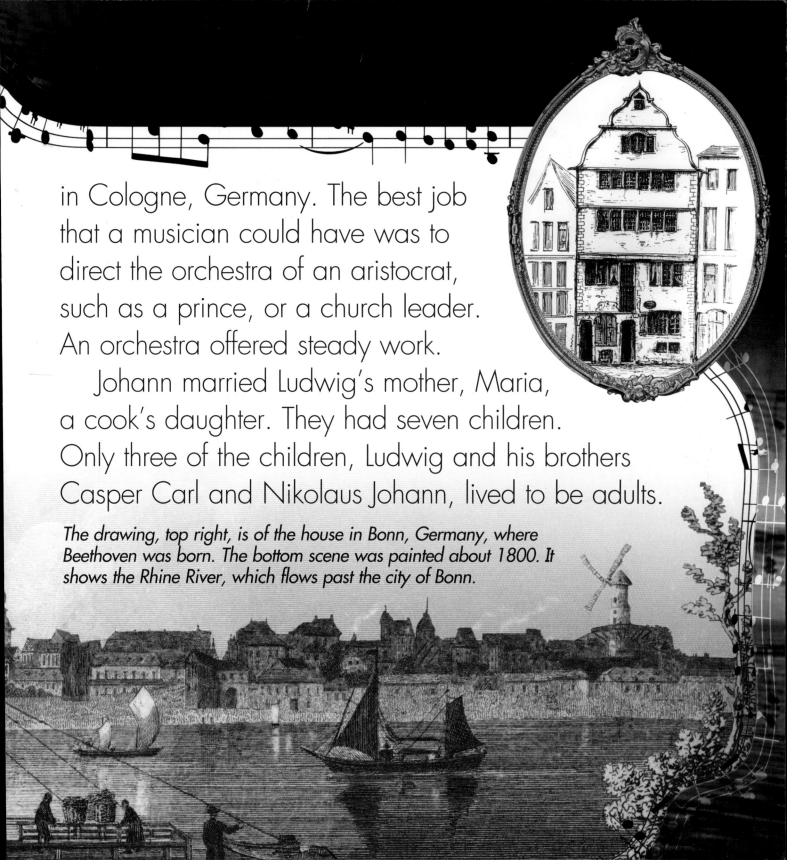

in Cologne, Germany. The best job that a musician could have was to direct the orchestra of an aristocrat, such as a prince, or a church leader. An orchestra offered steady work.

Johann married Ludwig's mother, Maria, a cook's daughter. They had seven children. Only three of the children, Ludwig and his brothers Casper Carl and Nikolaus Johann, lived to be adults.

The drawing, top right, is of the house in Bonn, Germany, where Beethoven was born. The bottom scene was painted about 1800. It shows the Rhine River, which flows past the city of Bonn.

Learning the Hard Way

Wolfgang Amadeus Mozart, who was 14 years older than Beethoven, was a famous musical **prodigy**. By age five Mozart had composed music and become a musician. He started **performing** at age six. Young Beethoven was not a prodigy, but his father wanted him to be. He began teaching Ludwig to play the **piano** and the **violin** when the boy was only four years old. Ludwig was so small that he could only reach the keys on the piano by standing on a piano stool.

Ludwig's father was not a kind teacher. He often locked Ludwig in the cellar and woke him up in the middle of the night to perform for guests. Johann even told his friends that Ludwig was younger than he was, so that Ludwig's playing would seem more special.

Ludwig spent only a few years in school. He did poorly at spelling and at math. He did like learning languages. In addition to German, his native language, he learned to read Latin, French, and Italian.

This portrait shows Beethoven as a young man. As a young boy, Ludwig preferred experimenting with musical notes to taking music lessons.

Making a Name for Himself

Beethoven first performed in front of an **audience** at a **concert** in Cologne in 1777, when he was seven years old. Three years later, he began taking **keyboard** lessons from Christian Gottlob Neefe, who was the chief organist in a court orchestra in Cologne. Neefe was a much kinder teacher than Ludwig's father had been. Ludwig wrote his own music, and Neefe helped him **publish** this music in 1783, so that other musicians could play it.

The next year, Ludwig was hired as a keyboard player and an assistant to the chief organist of the court orchestra. One year later, at the age of 14, he was **promoted** to second organist and was paid a full **salary**, just as the adult musicians were.

Beethoven had a special uniform when he performed with the court orchestra. He always wore a fancy green dress coat, silk stockings, a hat, and a sword with a silver strap.

Beethoven earned money for his family by giving piano lessons and small concerts. Here he is shown conducting the Razumovsky Quartet.

W. A. MOZART
geb. zu Salzburg d. 27t Jun. 1756, gest. zu Wien d. 5t Decbr. 1791

Don Juan, Zauberflöte, Figaro,
Entführung, Idomeneo,
Cosi fan tutte, Titus
Requiem

Sinphonien
Quartette
Varia-tionen.

L. van BEETHOVEN
geb. zu Bonn d. 17t Decbr. 1770, gest. zu Wien d. 26t März. 1827

Fidelio, Egmont, Christus am
Oelberge, Adelaide
Missa solennis.

Sonaten
Concerte

In 1787, Beethoven traveled to Vienna, Austria, to study with Mozart. Beethoven was 17, and Mozart was 31. When they met, Mozart thought Beethoven's keyboard playing was ordinary. However, he was surprised that Beethoven was able to improvise, or to compose music as he played it. Mozart told his friends, "Keep your eye on him. One day he'll give the world something to talk about."

Beethoven did not stay with Mozart for long. After two weeks, Beethoven got word from his father that his mother was ill. She died soon after Beethoven returned home. His baby sister Maria Margarethe died a few months later. The deaths made the family very sad, but Beethoven soon had other worries.

Beethoven and Wolfgang Amadeus Mozart are shown at the left. As did many other composers at the time, Beethoven studied with a more experienced composer, Mozart, to better his abilities as a musician.

Back to Vienna

Saddened by his wife's death, Beethoven's father began to drink too much, and he had to spend many nights in jail. Beethoven became responsible for his family. He went back to his old job in the court orchestra and gave piano lessons to make money. Beethoven's father died just a few days after Beethoven's twenty-second birthday.

Count Ferdinand von Waldstein, a powerful man in Cologne, liked Beethoven's music. He made sure that Beethoven continued his musical studies. The count **persuaded** Beethoven's boss at the court orchestra to send him back to Vienna, and to continue paying him his salary. In Vienna Beethoven studied with composer Franz Joseph Haydn. The two men did not get along with each other. Beethoven preferred to skip Haydn's lessons and to study with other composers.

Beethoven played this piano, which is now in the Beethoven Museum in Bonn, Germany. Beethoven became a popular performer all over Europe.

The Symphony

Beethoven is most famous for his nine **symphonies**. The word "symphony" comes from a Greek word meaning "sounding together." A symphony is performed by musicians who play many different kinds of instruments. A conductor leads the orchestra. He or she makes sure that everyone plays at the right **volume**, or sound level, and at the right **tempo**, or speed. A symphony is usually divided into four parts, called movements. The first movement is often fast, and the second is usually slow. The third movement is often in a tempo meant for dancing. The end of the symphony usually has the most stirring music. The music in the fourth movement is upbeat, fast, and strong.

Beethoven composed symphonies that joined different movements, and he used loud **chords** to make the music more exciting.

This painting shows Beethoven at work composing music. He wrote music for instruments that had not been used in symphony orchestras before.

A Silent Tragedy

On April 2, 1800, Beethoven's first symphony was performed in Vienna. Emperor Francis I said, "There is something revolutionary [new and original] about that music."

In 1799, when Beethoven was 28 years old, he realized that he was losing his hearing. He tried many things to cure his condition. He swallowed certain pills, rubbed on special creams, and took cold baths. Nothing worked. For a while, Beethoven used "ear trumpets" to make sound flow into his ears. As his condition worsened, people wrote down what they wanted to say to him in "**conversation** books." By 1818, at age 48, Beethoven was totally **deaf**.

Beethoven still conducted his concerts even though he could not hear the orchestra. He tried to quiet the orchestra during the loud parts and waved his arms wildly during the soft parts. Beethoven never knew that another conductor had to stand behind him and secretly conduct so that the musicians would know what to do.

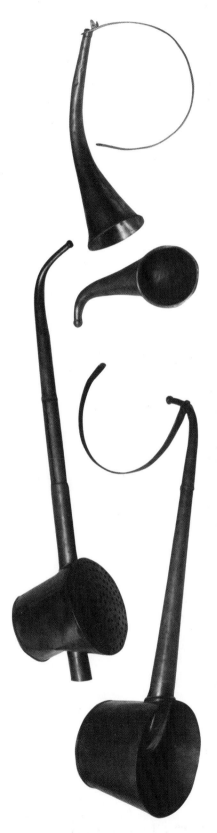

This picture of Beethoven was painted several years before he became deaf. As he lost his hearing, Beethoven also lost friends because he was often rude to people. Beethoven used these unusual-looking ear trumpets to help him to hear. They did not work very well.

The Heroic Symphony

In the summer of 1803, Beethoven started his third symphony, which he called the Bonaparte symphony, in honor of the French leader Napoléon Bonaparte. Napoléon had helped to lead the French people in their **revolution** against the French royalty. However, in May 1804, Napoléon crowned himself **emperor** and began to conquer several European countries. Beethoven felt that Napoléon had turned against everything that had made him a hero. He tore the title page of the symphony in half. When the new symphony was finally published in 1806, it was called the Eroica symphony, which means "heroic." On the new title page, Beethoven said the symphony was "to celebrate the memory of [the] great man" that Napoléon had once been.

When Great Britain's Duke of Wellington conquered Napoléon in 1813, Beethoven wrote his Battle symphony, called Wellington's Victory, Op. 91, in honor of the event.

Top: *Napoléon, emperor of France, is shown with a crown and a cape.*
Bottom: *These are pages from Beethoven's Eroica symphony.*

Beethoven's Strange Habits

Beethoven had an unusual appearance. He was short, but he had a very large head with wild hair. He thought more about writing good music than he did about keeping himself clean. Often his clothes would get so dirty, friends slipped into his room while he slept, took his dirty clothes, and gave him new ones. Beethoven seemed not to know the difference. He wrote music on the window shades. He poured water on his head, which spilled all over the floor, to stay awake late at night. **Landlords** disliked him. He was made to move every few months. Once Beethoven went for a walk in the country and got lost. When policemen found him, they did not believe he was really Beethoven. They felt that a great composer could not be so messy.

There have been many paintings made of Beethoven, both during his life and after his death. This painting shows Beethoven resting in a forest.

Beethoven never married, but he was almost always in love. Most of the ladies he liked either were married or were of a much higher social class than he was. After Beethoven died, a love letter that he wrote to his "**immortal** beloved" was found. Nobody knows who she was. In 1801, Beethoven wrote his beautiful Moonlight **Sonata** for Countess Giulietta Guicciardi, to prove that he loved her. This was one of 45 sonatas that he wrote.

Beethoven never had children of his own, but he helped to raise Karl, his brother Casper Carl's son, with Karl's mother. However, Karl did not always agree with the way that Beethoven wanted to raise him. He thought that his uncle was grumpy. Also, Beethoven wanted Karl to go to a university. Karl wanted to join the army. Karl eventually joined the army against his uncle's wishes.

The sheet of music for Moonlight Sonata was written in ink. This picture, created in 1815, is of Beethoven's love, Countess Giulietta Guicciardi.

Beethoven wrote Symphony No. 9, which some people consider his greatest work, when he was totally deaf. In the fourth movement, a **chorus** joins the orchestra by singing parts of "Ode to Joy," a poem by German poet Friedrich von Schiller. The symphony was performed for the first time on May 7, 1824. The audience cheered, but Beethoven could not hear them. A member of the chorus turned him around to face the audience so he could see how much they had loved the music. On March 25, 1827, Beethoven fell into a **coma**. The next evening, during a snowstorm, Beethoven opened his eyes as the house shook with the sound of thunder. It is said that he shook his fist at the sky and suddenly died. Beethoven was 56 years old. More than 20,000 people lined the streets of Vienna to see Ludwig van Beethoven's **funeral** march pass.

On March 29, 1827, crowds of people came out for Ludwig van Beethoven's funeral in Vienna, as is shown in this watercolor painting.

Beethoven Lives On

Today Beethoven's music is played and heard in concert halls, on the Internet, on radios, on CDs, and in the movies. Many movies use Beethoven's music, such as Disney's *Fantasia* and *Immortal Beloved*, which is a movie about Beethoven's love letter.

The first four notes of Symphony No. 5, which Beethoven called "**fate** knocking on the door," also spell out the letter *V* in **Morse code**. During **World War II**, the **Allied nations** used this symphony as a signal for victory. The "Ode to Joy" at the end of Symphony No. 9 is the anthem for the recently formed European Union. In 2003, an original manuscript of Symphony No. 9 sold for about $3.4 million. As Ludwig said, "There are and there will be thousands of princes. There is only one Beethoven."

Listening to Beethoven

Beethoven wrote 9 symphonies, 5 piano concertos and 45 sonatas. Now that you have read about Ludwig van Beethoven's life, you might enjoy listening to his music, some of which is listed below.

Symphony No. 3 in E-flat Major (Eroica)

This is the symphony that Beethoven wrote originally for Napoléon.

Symphony No. 5 in C Minor

This is the symphony that starts "ba-ba-ba-BUMM, ba-ba-ba-BUMM."

Symphony No. 9 in D Minor (Choral)

This Beethoven symphony ends with a chorus singing the "Ode to Joy" along with the orchestra.

Für Elise/Piano Concerto No. 5 (Emperor)

If you have taken piano lessons, you may recognize Für Elise. The Emperor concerto is the last piano concerto that Beethoven wrote.

Timeline

1770 Ludwig van Beethoven is born in Bonn, Germany.
1777 Beethoven performs in his first public concert in Cologne.
1784 Beethoven becomes assistant organist for a Cologne orchestra.
1787 Beethoven studies with Mozart in Vienna.
1799 The first signs of Beethoven's deafness appear.
1800 Beethoven composes Symphony No. 1.
1808 Beethoven completes Symphony No. 5 and Symphony No. 6.
1818 Beethoven becomes completely deaf.
1824 The audience cheers as Beethoven conducts his Symphony No. 9.
1827 Beethoven dies in Vienna on March 26.

29

Musical Terms

chords (KORDZ) Combinations of three or more notes played at the same time.

chorus (KOR-us) A group of people who sing together.

classical music (KLA-sih-kul MYOO-zik) Music in the style of the eighteenth and nineteenth centuries.

composer (kom-POH-zer) A person who writes music.

compositions (kom-puh-ZIH-shunz) Pieces of writing or music.

concert (KON-sert) A public musical performance.

concerto (kun-CHER-toh) Music created for an orchestra and one or more solo instruments.

keyboard (KEE-bord) An instrument that uses a set of keys, such as a piano or organ.

musicians (myoo-ZIH-shunz) People who write, play, or sing music.

orchestra (OR-kes-truh) A group of people who play music together.

organ (OR-gen) A keyboard instrument that makes music by driving air through pipes of different sizes.

performing (per-FORM-ing) Singing, dancing, acting, or playing an instrument.

piano (pee-A-noh) A keyboard instrument with small hammers that strike wire strings to make music.

sonata (suh-NAH-tuh) A composition for one to four instruments, one of which is usually a keyboard.

symphonies (SIM-fuh-neez) Long musical compositions written for orchestras.

tempo (TEM-poh) The speed at which a musical piece is played.

violin (vy-uh-LIN) A small instrument that makes sound by having a bow drawn over its strings.

volume (VOL-yoom) A measure of how loud or soft a sound is.

Glossary

Allied nations (A-lyd NAY-shunz) The countries that fought against the Axis powers in World War II. The Allies were Britain, Canada, China, France, Soviet Union, and the United States.

aristocrats (uh-RIS-tuh-krats) Members of the wealthy upper class.

audience (AH-dee-ints) A group of people who watch or listen to something.

baptized (BAP-tyzd) To have sprinkled someone with or to have lowered someone in water to show that person's acceptance into the Christian faith.

coma (COH-muh) A long period of unconsciousness.

conversation (kon-ver-SAY-shun) Talking.

court (KORT) The king or queen or other ruler's advisers and officers.

deaf (DEF) Not able or partly able to hear.

emperor (EM-per-er) The ruler of an empire or of several countries.

fate (FAYT) The power that supposedly decides what will happen in the future.

funeral (FYOON-rul) The service held when burying the dead.

immortal (ih-MOR-tahl) Living forever.

landlords (LAND-lordz) People who rent out rooms or space in their buildings.

Morse code (MORS KOHD) An alphabetical code, using dots and dashes, invented by Samuel F.B. Morse in 1837.

patron (PAY-trun) A person who gives money to support artists or musicians.

persuaded (per-SWAYD-ed) To have convinced someone to do something.

prodigy (PRAH-deh-jee) A child who is very smart and talented in some way.

promoted (pruh-MOHT-ed) To be raised in rank or importance.

publish (PUH-blish) To print something so people can read it.

revolution (reh-vuh-LOO-shun) A complete change in government.

salary (SAL-ree) A fixed amount of money paid to a worker.

World War II (WURLD WOR TOO) A war fought by the United States, Great Britain, France, and the Soviet Union against Germany, Japan, and Italy from 1939 to 1945.

Index

Primary Sources

Page 4. The oil-on-canvas portrait of Beethoven was painted by Joseph Carl Stieler, circa 1818–1823.

Page 5–6. An image of people on a jetty in *Bonn on the River Rhine*, painted circa 1800.

Page 6. The portrait of Beethoven's grandfather, Ludwig, is an oil on canvas portrait painted by Leopold Radoux, 1754–1781.

Page 7. Inset. A nineteenth-century French School engraving of Beethoven's birthplace in Bonn, Germany.

Page 8. Ludwig van Beethoven as a young man, oil on canvas, by the German School. Historisches Museum der Stadt, Vienna, Austria, eighteenth century.

Page 12. Double commemorative engraving of Wolfgang Amadeus Mozart and Ludwig van Beethoven, Museum der Stadt Wein.

Page 15. Photograph of a piano belonging to Beethoven, Beethoven Museum, Bonn.

Page 19. The oil-on-canvas portrait of Beethoven was painted by Willibrord Joseph Mahler (1778–1860). Historisches Museum der Stadt, Vienna, Austria.

Page 19. Hearing aids used by Beethoven. They were designed by Beethoven's friend Johann Nepomuk Maelzel, the inventor of the metronome.

Page 20. Eroica sheet music on which Beethoven erased dedication to Napoléon, leaving a hole in the paper. Gesllschaft der Musikfreunde, Vienna, Austria.

Page 20. Portrait of Napoléon Bonaparte by Appiani, Andrea the Elder (1745–1817). Kunsthistorisches Museum, Vienna, Austria.

Page 24. Photo engraving of Countess Giulietta Guicciardi from an anonymous drawing.1815, Beethoven Haus, Bonn, Germany.

Page 24. Score sheet of Moonlight Sonata in pen and ink on paper. Beethoven Haus, Bonn, Germany.

Page 27. Watercolor of Ludwig van Beethoven's funeral in Vienna, by Franz Stober (1760–1834). Beethoven Haus, Bonn, Germany.

Web Sites

Due to the changing nature of Internet links, PowerKids Press has developed an online list of Web Sites related to the subject of this book. This site is updated regularly. Please use this link to access the list: www.powerkidslinks.com/plfc/beethove/